NOISE.

NOISE.

a collection of poetry

ELLYS SMITH

Ellys Smith

For my mother, Patricia who has held my hand through the darkness.

My sisters, Brittany and Hannah always embraced me and taught me how to be strong.

My high school friends have walked with me through the fire of adolescence and fought my battles by my side.

And for those who destroyed me, crushed me, used me. You are the reason I am who I am today, although I wish I never met you I would never be this strong without

And for my dearest 11th-grade English teachers, Trevor Miller and Jane Gill

who pushed me to step outside my comfort zone and made me believe I was something.

You showed me I had something to say and taught me how to say it.

You made me feel comfortable in my pain and taught me how to turn all that pain into something beautiful.

I would not have written this if it were not for you.

Again, I want to dedicate a large part of this project to my mother for really inspiring me to go forward and take this chance and be vulnerable, she is my rock, and I wouldn't be a sliver of myself without her.

Copyright © 2023 by Ellys Smith

All rights reserved. No part of this book may be reproduced in any manner whatsoever without written permission except in the case of brief quotations embodied in critical articles and reviews.

First Printing, 2023

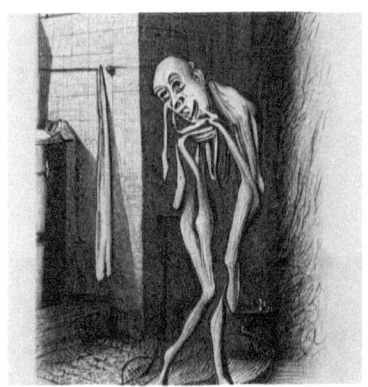

Noise. By Ellys Smith

Contents

<u>darkness 4 shame 3 5 LETTERS THAT never sent 6 7 growth 91</u>

This is the messy story of love and loss and the struggles of emerging from adolescence,

the joys and damages of relationships and discovering who you really are,

I hope my poetry can relate to those who have felt the same hurt.

My goal was to express all the things we are all so scared to say.

This book is dedicated to those who broke me, those who fixed me and

those who gave me a reason to stay.

For my mother, Patricia who has held my hand through the darkness.

For my sisters, Brittany and Hannah who always embraced me and taught me how to be strong.

For my high school friends that have walked with me through the fire of adolescence and fought my battles by my side.

And for those who destroyed me, crushed me, used me.

You are the reason I am who I am today, although I wish I never met you I would never be this strong without you.

And for my dearest 11th grade English teachers, Trevor Miller and Jane Gill

who pushed me to step outside my comfort zone and made me believe I was something.

You showed me I had something to say and taught me how to say it.

You made me feel comfort in my pain and taught me how to turn all that pain into something beautiful.

I would not have written this if it were not for you.

Again, I want to dedicate a large part of this project to my mother for really inspiring me to go forward and take this chance and be vulnerable, she is my rock, and I wouldn't be a sliver of myself without her.

Darkness.

"I don't want my scars to fade, they remind me too much of you."

I've run out of thoughts to think.
Words to say.
People to love.
I've lost control.
I'm so encompassed by my own emptiness, loneliness. Self-pity.
There's no happy ending for me.
No forever answers.
Or even a satisfactory feeling settled in my soul.
Nothing can complete me or fulfill me.
Why am I still so hungry?
And what is it that my stomach is missing.
It seems already so full, yet I am longing for something more.
It's never enough.
I am not enough for myself.
Give me more.
Please.
Just give me someone I can waste my days with.
When I'm lost.
It's so easy to go back to the darkness.
It's so comforting to be in pain.

You buried your damage and shame inside of me.
And I have had to carry it with me every day.
It is so fucking heavy.

I could not feel more lost right now
You tricked me, lured me into a game I could never win.
Was it worth it?
Was she worth it?
I thought for once I was given the chance to feel happy
You were my medicine
I felt so safe with you
I could genuinely waste every minute with you
You made me believe in something and then tore it away
I am devastated that I still crave you
I could get so lost in you
I miss the taste of your lips on mine
I miss the way you held me
I miss the way you smell
I miss the way time flew when we were together
Nothing lasts forever.
I just wish we had a better chance.
How to: ruin your own life.
You must become numb and reckless.
Become easily attached and keep your guard up.
Love too hard.
Get too hurt.
Forgive too easy.
Waste money you don't have on drugs to keep you sane.

Fantasize about dying while slowly killing yourself, with every cut, hit, drag, sip, burn.

We all die someday.

To live this life

You must give up everything

Lose all hope

Become completely separate from your body

Feel nothing and everything

Until it's too much to bear.

And you truly become nothing.

How draining: to hate the body you are born with.

To despise every line, curve, and flaw.

Everything I was made to embrace I am left with a hole that cannot be filled with self-love.

Trust me I want to feel joy when I see my reflection.

I want to accept myself and flourish in my individuality.

Yet, I still compare myself to everything I am not.

Tunnel vision of all the things I will never be.

I am a ball of insecurity, a collection of self-pity and tragedy.

A never-ending cycle that I do not know how to break.

It crushes me. Engulfs me. Destroys me.

Who am I, if not the list of traits I have mimicked of others?

Who am I when I am alone?

Who am I when I am lost?

Staying in that relationship,
Would have killed me.

You sexualise my pre-pubescent body.
Before I'd learned to hate it
Before you could break it
I've wanted you before
Back when we were nervous to hold each other's hands
I had no idea what level of damage you would cause.
Even still.
When I desire to be wanted by a man
I get to work on my garden.
Just to spark their interest.
In my child like body.
No hair.
No fat.
No wrinkles.
No cellulite.
"That's how they want you."
You want to make love to a child.
Not a **woman.**

I was born in a state of blame.

Accepting the fall.

Like when I finally take the jump off the interstate.

Taking each hit.

Like my mother on a Sunday night at dads.

I lived in a world that was my fault

Stepping on a crack in cement and coming home to a mother with cancer.

How do you fix what you didn't break?

Who told me?

I was to blame

Who points the finger at those limbless and numb?

As a kid when I did something wrong
My punishment was always physical
Now I punish myself with the same morals.
If I hate myself my only choice is to hurt myself.
Some traditions never change.

I pretended for so long that nothing happened to me
now I cannot stop thinking about it and there is nothing I can do to stop it.

I cannot stop it from happening to me.

I cannot stop myself from remembering.

I cannot stop myself from how I handled it.

Let it go.

Let the pain, fear, and sadness free.

I am more.

So much more.

Forgetting is not the answer.

Rising from the fear and becoming untouchable just might be.

I think that sometimes families are meant to be broken.
Sometimes the pain of that empty void you left,
Is better than the pain of two parents that just don't love each other
Anymore
There couldn't have been another way
Sometimes you have to choose your pain.

Winter.
I'm deep in a pit of depression
I can't climb out
I'm not eating
I'm not moving
I'm not taking care of my body
I am ignoring my mind.
I haven't brushed my teeth in days
I wonder if these blurry faces even notice
I pick at my scabs as I sob leaving black stains on my linen.
Sometimes I make myself get up
Though its rare.
Trying so desperately to end the cycle
I scrub hard.
Deep clean.
And brush my teeth until my gums bleed.
The sink fill with diluted blood.
I meet my reflection as I look down.
This reminds me of my nightmares.
I check my pulse to make sure I'm still here.
Then, I crawl right back into bed.
Winter is coming.
Which means more layers, to cover my scars.
Which means I'm more inclined to introduce new ones.

Growing out of fear

I'm lying awake another night. The wind from the cold air hovers over me as my restless eyes wander. Thinking back to all the times I forgave you for what you did.

I'm isolated in a world suffocated by people.

I can't hear myself think.

I can't even catch my breath.

Every night you drink is another night you will regret.

Blinded by your own actions you don't see the pain you cause.

Nothing I do is good enough for you.

I'm far too lost.

The house shakes with every slam of your fist, those same hands that held me tight and told me my love was safe with you.

Once my guardian angel filled with joy,

Now nothing but a blood thirsty pathetic decoy.

I can't escape you.

No matter how hard I try, I always find my way back.

I close my eyes and try to dream of where the sun and stars will take me far away.

Where I will never have to see your face.

But I wake up, to no flowers or trees.

No sunshine or cool breeze.

It was a dark winter, where violence stole the night.

You fed on our fears like a monster,
Helpless you had no mercy on us.
I was no longer living.
Even my mind was a prison.
I have never felt so weak.

Until someone came into my life, and they looked so much like you.

I thought it was loving just the same.

You taught your little girl to believe love was painful.

I fall in love so quickly

Give myself over instantly

I want to be held so badly that

I don't even consider what kind of impact the fall will have

I am so eager to find love

That I blindly accept sorrow in its place

My hope continually weighing me down.

This week I'm obsessed with a boy that I won't even remember.

That I really know nothing about.

But I will probably dream about him.

Build a perfect world in my mind.

That disappears when I open my eyes.

I think my need for being loved

outweighs my need for another person to complete me.

I need someone to prove to me that I matter

That **I am fucking needed by someone.**

Everybody is moving and I am stuck in place
I have no true meaning
I think maybe I was put here to fill space,
To fill time.
A side story.
A crossed path.
Who am I?
Who am I?
Who am I?

3:07am –
why the fuck am I still awake.
I didn't sign up for this.
I just want to close my eyes.
And disappear. Just for a few moments.
I can't escape this world of danger and tragedy.
Even in my sleep I can't escape my past.
It is eating me alive.

White sheets-stained red.

To speak is to find vulnerability.
To express the deepest parts of yourself.
Is it worth all the pain?
To speak is to break.
So, I will keep my mouth tapped.

I think I lost a very big part of myself when my grandmother died.

I never told anyone how bad it hurt.

This part of life I accepted too quickly.

And I've left the grieving to an older sadder version of who I used to be.

I wish I spent more time with her.

I wish I didn't show up too late.

I wish she could have hugged me back one last time.

I wish. I wish. I wish.

It's too late for wishes.

Let.

Her.

Go.

My father never hit me; but.
He made sure I knew he could.
Why was I the only one.
The guilt. The shame I felt.
Coward.
Hiding in the shadows, staying out of the way.
Brace for impact. I can still hear them crying.
Suddenly I'm six again, under the stairs feeling my brother hit every stair above as he begs for his life to be over, so he never has to see my father again.
I get it.
I have no right to forgive him on behalf of his victims.
I'm just a coward.
With no voice.
I learnt the power of silence at a very young age.

That couch has seen so much

It has held those we have loved and lost

It has seen every season of this home.

That couch has held many lovers, many enemies, many spills across the fabric.

That couch was there for every laugh, tear, fight, celebration.

You've been there through it all dear friend.

You sat beneath me for my first kiss.

The first time I said I love you,

To someone who didn't know how to handle with care

You were there when the boy that didn't love me

spread me open and poured out all of his sins inside my sacred soul

and left without a trace.

It always goes back to him.

Why did he have to ruin that couch?

He took away everything.

I thought my couch could always be mine.

You took away so much from me that night.

For some reason,
I always seek the attention of older men.
I want to be that only exception.
I want to be the "just this once."
I want to be beautiful in a timeless way.
I want to make a man feel young again.
Let me forever be your fountain of youth.
Drink me until there's nothing left.

I fall in love with everyone that feeds me the attention I am so hungry for
I love being loved
I love, loving people
I do not think I have ever had movie love
But I have loved quickly, I have loved messy
And I have loved deeply
I often choose the ones that love to tear me in two
I love being broken – being torn apart and having to repair myself from nothing again
I love the pain of it all
I am the broken pieces that do not get picked off the floor
I am the glass shard that you cannot seem to get out
I am the pain, the sorrow, and the misery
I am the person everyone wants to experience once
Everybody wants to watch the fire burn, but nobody ever wants to stay to put it out.

I'm dangerous,
Baby. I'm cool.
I bet you've never tasted someone like me.
Give me a try.
I carry the weight of the world on my shoulders,
Hold the bruises on my feet from the miles I've travelled running away.
Blood drips down my sleeves.
I'm sorry if I've made you uncomfortable.
I know the way I look doesn't reel you in
But I promise I'm worth it
I'm sorry this scares you
I'm sorry you don't know what it's like
I'm sorry this must be a lot to handle.
Just put my picture on the wall, give your thanks and wish me well.
I'm gone.

Sometimes I wonder if my mother is proud of who I am becoming.

When I undress myself
I still feel you staring
When I cry alone encompassed by the wind
There you are smiling, laughing at me.
When I love another,
I feel you in their place, and I remember I'll never be safe being vulnerable with another.

When I eat, I still hear your voice telling me I've had too much.

I feel you everywhere
There is no escaping you.

Be good.
Always be good.
do what he wants.
Good girl is small.
Good girl stays quiet
Good girl does not get in trouble
Everybody loves good girl
Shes perfects
Golden hair, contagious smile, eyes as blue as the ocean, she is good.
She does what she is told
She does not complain
I thought I had to be like good girl.
Anything to make you happy.
Good girl lives everyday like its improv moving with the phrase "yes, and?"
"Do you want to sleep with me?" he says.
Good girl is not ready at fifteen.
Good girl says nothing.
Good girl stays quiet and takes it.
Good girl does not feel so good about herself anymore.
By the time He is done with her, she has lost all feeling, her eyes heavy from all the sobbing.
He says "good girl"
I thought this is what you wanted.

Good girl is just a girl now.

Nothing special.

Girl never tells.

Girl lets him destroy her

Girl is "fucking crazy" because she cuts herself and needs therapy now.

Nobody wants to be like girl anymore or help girl or save girl.

She is no fucking good.

The things that are killing me.

Are the only things that are seeming to keep me alive.

shame.

"I've been hiding from myself for so long I have forgotten what I look like."

You promised me love and grace
I was certain that you were my safe place
Hidden from the light, you are all I can see
But if the sun is stolen
How do I know that I am free?
I am chained to the floor
Or I am suffocated by the sheets
I do not even know what is out there waiting for me
If you love someone let them go
Even when I am gone, you will find a way to show

Alone
Water dripping down my body
I crumble
My safest place is the floor of my bathtub
I let it seep in
I let it sting
I like the pain
It is my favourite thing

- There is nothing like that instant gratification

  Time is passing
  days turn to weeks
  weeks turn to months
  months into years
  <u>life is all just a blur with nothing to show for myself</u>

I'm so exhausted by the one thing I love.
the one thing I can rely on.
my paper, my pen.
The words of my soul spilling out endlessly.
Where is my voice.
What do I have to say?
I sit I stare I wish a had something to share.
I stand jealous of the magic hat with never ending ideas

that used to flow.
Now I'm stuck with the same old metaphors and similes.
I call myself a poet.
What a lie.
I'm constantly pretending to be something I'm not.

I've been the child to many people I call parent
The lover of many sleepless nights
I've been the mother to many poorly raised sons
The dreamer of many unattainable goals
I have been cold outside just trying to get warm
I've accepted love that looked too much like abuse
And begged to be loved by somebody
Countless times
I keep getting what I ask for
But never in the right way
- I'm waiting for somebody to love me right.

I've been an empty shell of a person these last few days
I hate everything that keeps me alive
I want to rebel
I'm avoiding being sober at all costs.
I can't be alone with my thoughts.
My brain is my biggest enemy
It's my fault
It's all my fault
There has to be something wrong with me.

you take the food of my soul and devour every lick
you disgust me
you think because you can control me because you tried to eat me alive
there's nothing I can do to stop you
you've made me so weak
you think that you have won because you invoke fear
I won't budge.
You can't scare me.
No matter how many times you bombard me, chase me, catch me.
I will not be afraid.
I will be loud.
I will rumble.
You will not hurt me again.
The crumbs left of who I am will always be more filling
Then every bite of you.
You are nothing.
So dry.
So empty.
So, fucking lost.
My hope in you will never fade
after everything you have done to me
I still need you
-fatherless

5:26 am
Today I decided to take my meds
I filled up my water bottle,
After filling my lungs with smoke.
And placed three of my devilish mood stabilizers on my tongue
And sipped out of my straw.
The water was hot.
Scolding almost.
How did I miss it?
You would assume in seventeen years on earth I'd know which side
turned my faucet cold.
My mind must be slowly deteriorating.

You thought it would hurt me to see how I replaceable I was
Truth is,
I was sad to see how incapable you were of growth
Though.
I was not surprised.

If only I could still, ask my grandma for advice.
I still miss her so much.

One time I kissed a boy,
Because he wanted me too.
He wanted to touch me,
So, I let him.
I didn't know what I was supposed to want.
I didn't think I would remember the way his hands felt tracing every piece of me.
I didn't think I would regret showing him the parts of me I don't even see.
I just feel wrong.
Something about the way we loved wasn't right.
I don't know what I could have done differently.
This has been on my mind a while.
How do I get rid of the shame of past lovers?

There is nothing like that first time.
Knowing that's the last time you will ever experience that for the first time.
Kind of ruins it.
I think.

They want me to be sick.

This is what they call beautiful.

The cold shivers, the thinning hair, the yellow teeth.

This is what you want?

Heroin chic? Because this body must appeal to your trends?

They love us sick girls.

Girls they can fix, girls they can control.

Everything they want we give.

We are conducted to love others.

We pour everything into them because we will never be that for ourselves.

Why do we fall for these traps?

I love performing.

I love to act and pretend.

I love the drifting into another mind, escaping my reality for just a moment.

I adore the show.

The feeling of doing a good job.

What it's like to be adored.

To be praised.

I do it for the smiles.

If you're happy so am I.

I mimic feelings, emotions, reactions.

I reflect exactly what you want to see.

Where is my applause?

My standing ovation?

Did I do a good job?

It is my fault for believing you wanted me
for anything more than my body

I don't let myself spend time alone anymore
I don't let the voices tell me what to do
I must hide from them in your arms
Keep me safe from myself
Hear my cries and tell me I'm not alone
Tell me you have voices too
Let me hear them
Let me talk to them
Let me in

Routine of self-deprecation.
I stand in front of my dirty mirror.
Turn the faucet to scolding.
Waiting as the air grows thick.
And sweat drips down my chin.
I'm so still.
Staring at my reflection as the mirror grows foggier and foggier.
I stare until I am completely unrecognizable.
I wish this was all they could see.
I wish I could hide forever.
I step into the burning shower.
And collapse to the floor.
This is where I do my best work.
This is the place where all misery come to play.
Where dark thoughts run rampant.
Where urges strike me like the match I want to light to this skin.
This is where I should find my peace.
This is where my soul goes to rest.
Be quiet while she sleeps.

A letter to my 15-year-old self,
I am sorry.
Sorry, for pretending like he didn't hurt you.
Sorry, for never telling anyone what he did to you.

Your story is real.
Your story matters.
It is not your fault.
It is not something to be embarrassed of.
And you should never hold that shame.
You don't have to move on.
You don't have to grow up.
You don't have to be quiet.
You can be as angry as the waves swallowing a ship filled with those who never believed you.
You can also be at peace.
The bad doesn't have to control your life.
There is so much more to you than what happened.
You are so much more than the pain.

Hunger

The numbers are overwhelming my mind
I do not know who I am anymore
I am nothing but the numbers on the scale
My worth is dependant on my success rate
If I eat today, I will hate myself
Until the day when I am nothing
I want to be weak and fragile
Delicate And soft
If I am not small, I am not a woman
I need to be smaller
I need to be nothing

I wish I could want me for you.
But I do not even want myself.
I crave your validation.
The taste of danger on your tongue.
your arms pulling me closer to your embrace.
I felt so safe within your touch.
I miss those fleeting moments we shared.
Even though you are not mine,
Jealousy consumes me like a raging fire.
I want you so bad.
My heart burns for you.
This "love" is the house,
that I have set my match to.
Yet you have carelessly escaped.
Why must you avoid the burn.
Why will not you stay warm with me.
I am trapped within my own disaster.
Alone, engulfed by the flames.
My lungs filled with smoke.
Flesh into bones.
But I feel nothing.
Because you are not here.

The fog in my brain goes black
Thick air clouds my vision.
I have no control.
Fantasizing of who I should have been,
And dreading who I am.
I convinced myself that my only outlet was pain.
The stinging water on my fragile skin relieves me.
Destroying my body to match the emotional damage you caused.
I have to hurt myself before anyone else can.
When you hate your brain,
And you hate your body.
All you can feel is trapped and suffocated.
My only escape is pain.
I need another way.
So, I write.
I Write shitty poems without context.
Hoping someone will reach out a hand and pull me up for air.
At least I've advanced from blades on flesh to being consumed by the rhythm of my pen on paper.
Instead of blood dripping down my body,
I watch the blood of ink seep into my pages.
And instead of waking up wishing I hadn't.
I'm letting my past free,

And holding on for the future
Because I'm realizing
I really don't want to let go.
I am filled with rage
Nobody knows what you did to me
Nobody would believe me
This system has failed so many lost souls
How do I prove what you stole for it is something you cannot see?
My innocence, the light in my eyes
Women too scared to speak up
Daily we are forced to see the men that destroy us
And were expected to do nothing
Nothing but letting the pain engulf me
But what can I do?
It is just boys being
Boys.

I was replaceable
I was easy to forget
But I will always remember how you made me feel
How you took the deepest secrets of mine and turned them into flaws
You made me ashamed of myself
You took away the best parts of me and made them yours
You took my innocence
And made me hand myself to you
You pushed me under till I could no longer breathe
I was suffocating
Slowly you would give me air
Then force my soul below the surface
I had to find the strength
To let go
To breathe
I had to allow myself to find comfort in the darkness
I am new again
You thought you could break me
And take all I was but I am unstoppable
I am a champion of my own defeats
And I survived you
One day you will get your karma
And watch me thrive
One day you will realize what you did to me

And drown all alone
In an ocean of regret that you created

Touch

My body is no longer my own
My fingers trace my jagged skin
And all that comes to mind
is your name
What had been stolen from me, I cannot replace
Flashbacks burning in my mind
like the most desirable flame
I wish I had known how wrong it was
for you to touch me
For you to shed my layers
and bury yourself inside me
So, when I hold myself
Touch myself,
Embrace myself,
I am reminded of how clearly,
I am no longer my own.

The R word.

When I say, I was raped. It sounds like it was my fucking fault.

Emphasis on I right? Because I had to do something to deserve it right?

when the moment replays over and over in my mind, I am obsessed.

when I say I want to kill myself because I don't know how to live with the fear that is planted in me, I am crazy.

So, I will be the crazy bitch that got raped.

Because what he did to me sticks with me.

I see It everyday. I feel him holding me down.

I feel the tears running down my face because I want it to stop.

I want everything to stop.

When I see him at school, walking past me, laughing, living despite it.

I am so fucking jealous.

He gets to live.

And I am just fucking crazy.

Fucking crazy for being trapped in the body you broke.

Trapped being 15 on my couch.

I would give anything to go back and take care of that girl.

that did not know that it was not okay for him to touch her when she did not want him to.

She did not know how much it would hurt to continue living after him.

I also want to forgive her for all the times she did not believe the pain.

I want to love her for all the people that did not love her enough.

Red
Red was never my favourite colour
But I have been seeing a lot of it lately
Now I cannot seem to get enough of it
For some, the colour red is just the colour red.
But for me it is a feeling
It is a state of mind
It is dark
And painful
Yet nearly relieving
I cannot go a day without seeing red
It haunts me like passionate guilt
That I cannot live without
The water stings because of red
I am bombarded with questions because of red
I hide myself because of red
I hate myself for loving red.

Desires
Why don't you want me anymore?
I stare through you
Hoping you meet my gaze
But you never do
I would erase everything about myself for your validation
My obsession is spiralling
I want nothing more than your touch

Jealousy engulfs me like a raging wildfire
I want to be your everything
Yet I am still not even a something
I picture what we could have been
But I was nothing more than a regretted sin
If I had not handed myself to you so willingly
Our chances would not be so slim
Do you think I am easy?
Do you whisper slut as I pass you by?
Do you tell your friends about everything I did for your love?
My self-esteem is low
You only like me for my body
I am something to use
Something to play with
That is all I am worth
Nothing but skin and bones
I have been looking for love in all the wrong places
I crave being unwanted
I crave the curiosity of how
I could have met your expectations
I crave the chase.

Dear abuser,

You were my "first love"
I fell hard.
Your charm had swept me off my feet.
I could not think straight.
Thought it was normal to feel this way.
Made me believe I was nothing without you.
That I was so lucky to have you in my grasp.

I hated when I upset you.
So, I did everything **you** wanted.
When u said I was too big,
I could not touch a meal for weeks.
When I was no longer beautiful to you,
I dug deep beneath the layers of my flesh.
And when you could not hear my cries for help.
My pain.
I began to find comfort in my sorrow.
When I screamed no.
Yet you pushed me down and took away all I had left.
I was broken in every way.
At fifteen.

I thought love was merely satisfying your partner at your own expense.

I normalized it.
I catch your glimpse in the hall,
And you do not even know,
The pain you put me through.
The hell I endured alone.
So, there you are flourishing in your own ignorance
As I wither away, I am nothing.

Craving a sick body

I want to have a body that worries people

I want a body that is so fragile you could blow on it and id fall to my knees

A body that isn't too big for anybody
This need for sickness
What is it about?
What is wrong with me

I'm always fighting with myself

Waging a war between good and evil

I can't continue telling people to love themselves for who they are

While I spend all my time fantasizing about a deadly lifestyle.

Dreaming of being sick enough.

Losing my hair

Losing my period

Losing my mind

I'm glorifying suicide

Dreaming of sickness isn't something you do if you're okay.

Letters that never sent.

"I will inevitably lose myself loving you or lose you loving myself."

D,

My sweet forbidden fruit

You inspire me and change my grip on reality

I find my mind wandering to visions of you

You've replaced my foggy void with a heart that only beats for you

I remember our first kiss

So passionate

So endless

So intense

I wish it hadn't been our last.

I wish I knew I wanted you sooner

Now it's too late

My heart loses that beat you gave me

Why must everyone see what I see in you

So charming

You've turned me into a romantic.

Spending my time Thinking about how you look at me

Thinking about your smile

I'm desperate to lose all the noise and be comforted by only your soft whispers.

You slip away

It's all in my head

You belong to everyone and no one.

M,
I felt your heartbeat
And watched as you took your last breath
The warmth leaves your body
And heard your final words
That moment so vivid
And I am reminded by you in everything I do
The birds hum to the sound of your voice
And cloud's part with the sun when I say your name
Nothing could ever replace your love
And everything I do makes me think of you
I still feel you here
If your god is real
I hope that you are being taken care of
I hope the god you dedicated your life to loves you
I hope your god forgives me for hating him
I hope your god lets me see you again
Because why am I here if I do not have you.
C,
I must confess
In every song I sing
All I think of is your name
Your smile and quick remarks
Your dangerous flame that is spread to my heart
There is not a moment you are not in my mind.

Nothing but you.
Nothing that could out do or replace you.
Putting me first like never before
Never felt as beautiful as when you speak to me
I cannot help but think, this one going to hurt
I cannot let go; I only want you.
My sweet obsession.
My fiery desire.
I feel so intensely I can no longer breathe.
You are my only reason.

H,
You introduced me to all the coolest things
You tortured me and nurtured me
You were always my safety blanket
I knew when I was cold, you'd always be there to warm me up.
You made it easy to be poor
Meaning even when we were, I didn't feel it
You filled my life up with love, art, music, laughter and freedom.
When I was a kid
I wanted to be you
But I realize now that I could never fill your shoes
You are brave
And compassionate
And determined
You have turned many storms into sunshine
In this thing we call life.
J,
I rely on your warmth at night
The comfort of your shoulder to cry on.
I lay awake awaiting your call that you will save me from the dreadful fall.
You always save me from myself.
You give me a reason to make it through the day.

I'm sorry that I will never find enough love to repay you with.

I'd give you my life.

Because you are the reason for it.

I love you

I believe in the possibility of recovery because of you.

I hope that someone finally gives you the love you deserve.

If I could get you the world I would.

I would do anything for you.

The night before I fall
As I hover over the edge
Thinking of what's led me to this moment I feel my lips quiver and bones shake
Clenching my fists against the railing
Even with my rapid heartbeat and racing thoughts
I feel as if I could be making a mistake
I want to disappear
I want to evaporate into the air you breathe
Like I was never there
Like I'm nothing but a memory
Is it crazy for me to feel this way?
That life is a pointless journey of despair and heartache
Is it so wrong for me to vanish?
But even before this day I think
"am I prepared to be forgotten?"

D,
Thank you for showing me a mirror
A reflection
Thank you for showing me that you felt this too
And that you made it out
Thank you for seeing my scars.
Because nobody else wanted to talk about them.
Thank you for breaking my walls.
Thank you for sharing your darkness.
I love you.
You saved me.
Somehow when you came into my life
Light followed.

S,
You uplift me, Keep me young.
You bring light into every room.
You're so bright.
I grow jealous of your carefree nature.
You're so head strong, So confident.
I aspire to be like you.
I love you dear friend.
No one can make me laugh like you.
How special to have someone know you inside and out.
You were the first person I told.
First person that I wasn't scared of what they might say.
You accepted my damage with open arms.
You held my hand and destroyed all threats to my character.
You defend me and protect me.
You are my guardian angel and I adore you.
I don't want to know what life looks like without you.
I don't want to breathe any air that isn't yours.

I look below me at a body of water
And I think about how peaceful it would be
How quiet.
To be submerged.
The only sound being my heartbeat as the waves rush over me.
The only pain, being from those that left me scarred.
Drowning feels like a luxury.
My tears are nothing but water.
My pain is nothing but fear.
A stone wall built up so high,
It could never be climbed.
But stone gets so heavy.
Gravity only has but one instinct
And I am pulled
Farther
And farther,
Beneath the surface.

Was I not enough,
Could I have made you stay?
If only you did
Maybe I wouldn't have turned out this way
Watching you leave
Left scars on my heart
Without you
I'm broken
Dad.

Grandma.
What is there to live for
When the one person
You loved more than life itself
Is gone.

L,
I've never loved anyone the way I love you
It's a platonic eternal love.
I was bound to find you; you were meant to change my life.
Without you I wouldn't be me.
There would be half of myself never knowing what is missing.
We are so different yet so much brings us together.
Our brokenness that is only intact when we are together.
If I lost you, I'd lose myself, not only the parts of me you bring out, but I'd lose whatever I had to begin with.
When you cry, my heart aches.
Your pain is my pain, I feel it deep within my soul.
When I'm with you I feel complete, no longer filled with hate or shame, nothing but love.
You are love. Passion. The purest form of adoration.
Twin flame, partner in crime, forever intertwined.

K,
We bond over substance abuse and broken homes.
I love you and I can't let go
I'm lost
I'm spiralling
I can't get you out of my head
I can't get enough of you
I must watch from the outside as you love another
Destroying myself for all the reasons I am not her.
I picture your hands on my face never letting go
I can't lose you
You are the only one that really gets me
Maybe we're too alike
Maybe we're both a little too broken
And maybe we aren't ever going to be able to fix each other.

P,
The ashy winter
Where my heart no longer withers
I caress the skin that was given to you
Stare into the oceans you hold within your eyes
"The windows to the soul"
But my dear those windows have been shut for awhile
In denial in hopes for a better trial
But you are isolated
Trapped within your own misery
Hiding behind your troubled past
So, no one can see the damage
I see through
I see you.
I see the moments of black and blue
I see the decades of "I don't know anymore"
I also see the will to persevere
I see all the times you stayed
Stayed for the ones you love
stayed for me
Thank you for all the times you could have left
And you did not.

R,
My eyes open slowly to an image of perfection
Where the person I have been endlessly chasing
Is right there in front of me
You whisper softly, tender words into my ear
I have never heard something so beautiful
If I believed in love this would be it
I am staring directly into your calm brown eyes
Mesmerized by every detail, every flaw
You amaze me
When I am with you my heart is the sun at the break of dawn
My soul rejoices
This is the first time I have felt something in a while
I am pulling you in closer because I cannot get enough of your scent
The obsession is spiraling
It is out of control
I am out of control
I will not be satisfied until I have you
The light has shed
It is far too dark to see
That I'm merely skin and bones
From this trap I will never be free
I pick and pull at my skin

Like I could ever get a break
The scale shouts worthless
I could be so easily replaced
In a disassociated state
My eyes see things I cannot shake
If only I was smaller maybe you'd have stayed
Base my worth of standards that are nothing but fake
I dot the I's cross the T's. am I finally complete?
Make sure to reach your standards
But the bar is so damn hard to reach
Sexualized in my sweater I wear to hide my scars
They notice all the wrong things.
Could you save me? I think I've gone too far.

"Sweetie just smile you are lucky you're so blessed; you get what you get there's no reason to be upset."

But gifts don't make up for absence, money doesn't cloud the abuse

These lies and tricks are just distractions.
The words I love you are barely true.
I hide in my room, Screen fade to black
Isolated from the world, physical touch is something I lack.
Know when to be quiet and never see.
Daddy said being yourself makes you weak.
Nobody wants a girl like you
Just shut up and let the adults speak.
My fight or flight kicks in when I hear the screams.
Except I can't move. I simply freeze.
This can't be real, take me back to my dreams.
Where there's a prince and the sun and nice breeze.

Overwhelming damage caused from you inflicting pain with ease

Observing the wreckage of your emotions was like living I life with no sun.

Secrets are merely secrets, battle have barely begun

Holes in the walls and bruises on our cheeks.

This is not living; we are existing beyond extremes.

At eight years old praying to god, I don't wake up once I'm asleep.

Because another day causes so much more pain.

I'm going insane.

I can't handle all of the shame

Trapped in my brain.

Suffocated by skin.

Skin that is no longer mine

Since you let yourself in.

I scratch, cut, burn.

Trying to escape.

My body is a vessel in torturous grace.

D,
Her eyes meet mine across the room.
Stalking each other, not saying a word.
What game are we playing my love?
Everything about her is heaven.
What is my identity?
What are my desires?
While I catch myself admiring her beauty and her silhouette is on my mind.
The steaming hours of night when not a soul is in sight.
You are stunning.
You take my breath away.
I want you.
My first.
My only.
Your beauty has opened a door I did not know existed.
It feels so wrong to love you.

R,
You drive me crazy.
You make me wild.
Wish I could live without that daring smile.
For all the days you leave me bare.
I am going crazy.
please do not stare.
My mind is grey.
Sleeves-stained red.
I just cannot get you out of my head.
Last night I put a hole in my wall.
When you said it was over on our call.
When I see you.
I am filled with rage.
Why will not you love me.
Why will not you stay.
I want to hold you for a while.
I am insane.
I am in denial.

You were the one that got away,
The one they thought would stay.
The one I never considered might just be afraid.
Afraid of me or what I may become.
Afraid of all the feelings you've never accepted.
Fear of yourself or who you used to be.
Fear that the resurfacing of your mistakes may destroy you.
I've been there too.
My scars have seen the light.
My body has been shown,
My book is open for all to read.
And I'm not afraid anymore.
One day you'll accept it too.
It's okay to hold that fear in your stomach,
Just make sure to keep your pride in your socks
Don't let them take that away from you.
Not ever.
K,
I love your smile.
More so when I am the reason behind it.
I want to touch you, reach out and just hold you.
Were so fucking close yet we could not be more far apart.
You consume my mind.
Racing thoughts.
Let me indulge in you.

I am not jealous of what you two have.
I know deep withing I need you and you need me.
I beg god to let me have you.
I simply do not deserve you.
Shes everything you have wished for.
But I know you.
Really know you.
I feel you.
I understand you.
I dream that one day we may collide.
Beautiful wreckage of our love.
I have lost count of the pills.
And still nothing gets me as high as your love.

Growth.

"You hold me in your arms until I am able to carry myself."

Blade.
Sharp and gruesome, detailed, and exact.
You release me, you destroy me.
I will never forget the first time we met.
So mysterious, my curiosity spiralled.
Line after line.
My skin cries.
Beautifully arranged in overwhelming ways.
I think about you often, I cannot see you anymore.
Temptation rises.
Sobriety is difficult, but so is the pain.
So, when I call your name, do not answer.
Let me grieve without you.
Let me move on to something new.
Because all though I love you, you are tearing me apart.
You are stealing me from myself, Invading my mind.
Leaving your trace on my body.
I have had enough.

Today I am writing in red pen, today I am wanting to break the rules,

Today my teacher said write in pencil

Today I took control.

Every day I wait for my grades written in the ominous red.

We associate these feelings with colours,

Red is fear, darkness, anger, and tragedy.

I am starting to feel red everywhere.

I like to water it all down like its nothing while I work myself to the bone.

Somehow if I tell myself enough times ill believe it.

That is not true though.

There's comfort in the honesty, even if it hurts.

I would rather hate myself and know it then try to pretend I love who I am all the time.

You cannot always be perfect.

Sometimes you just got to be *red*.

A hundred times a day I think of how I will please you

A hundred times a day I defeat myself because I'll never compare

A hundred percent of my time wasted on being perfect

But yet you test me as if those are the numbers that define my worth

I've started to believe they do

What about the number of times I almost left but stayed?

Or the times I've loved and lost

Or the countless wars I've battled within me

Nobody sees.

You cast these stones, but you are blind to your own baggage

24 hours in a day

8 hours to rest if I'm lucky

To escape the chaos, escape the repetitive cycle

Yet I lie awake each night filled with anxiety and the burden of standards I have to meet.

Because the numbers define me.

Your condescending words define me.

The shame of never being able to compare defines me.

I want to mean something; I want to make a difference.

I have so many dreams for such a small person.

I want to matter, but how does one make a difference in such a selfish world.

You pile on the workload. Its weighing me down.

Leaving me to crumble with nothing but the scraps of effort I have left.

I'm silently drowning reaching for a hand.

You mistake that for weakness, you push me down pouring more water over me like the ocean I was drowning in wasn't enough.

You call me lazy, but this is all I have.

You don't see the layers behind my smile, the stress of being alive is draining enough.

Tear me down and expect me to pick up the pieces and be strong enough to take everything you throw at me.

But I'm left with nothing but the air in my lungs and I'm running out of breath.

This is not living.

I am destroying myself to meet your standards.

It's a funny game we play.

Pretending were all not secretly dying inside.

You praised this god as if they could protect you.
But how could they let this happen.
Her once admirable voice, shut down in an instant.
So vividly I remember his hands on her precious mouth.
Hands knotted behind her back. Helpless.
And so was I.
Locked with the isolated walls of my mother's car.
No choice to watch her in agony.
I found out what hatred was that day.
That feeling.
In the pit of my stomach
Heartbeat racing, eyes filled with wells of sadness.
My hands glued to the glass, shouting at the top of my lungs
Praying he'll hear me and let her go.
The purest of angels couldn't have saved her that day
My mind has chosen to forgive so many of the things you've done to us,
But the way you stole her strength remains in my memory.
It's as if I felt the bomb of your fist right there with her.
Tethered emotionally at a distance.
Distilled with fear at such a ripe age.
Never able to look at my father the same.
All I wish is to go back and save her,
My mother has taken every hit this world has had to offer me
She is my guardian angel.

She is the reason I have hope in the good.

I washed all the clothes you touched me in.
They still don't feel the same.
I forgot the way you said my name.
Dyed my hair blue because you loved it blonde.
Started cutting myself again because you already destroyed my softness.
Starved myself because I was never woman enough for you anyway.
I changed everything you loved.
You betrayed me for something better.
No one can ever hurt me the way you hurt me.

Antiques.

The traffic filled drive builds my anticipation as I count the minutes on my hand until we arrive and rush to the door in the blistering cold. I'm welcomed by the scent of a fresh meal and a warm embrace from my grandmother.

I stare at the familiar pictures on the beige walls that hold all the beautiful moments of my grandmother's life. Every memory remains withing these walls, not a crack or crease in sight. They bring me comfort, knowing sadness will never consume me here. This is my safe place. My safe people. It was my grandmother that made that place a home. Her radiant soul lit up every inch of that dull lifeless condo.

Everything was so clean and precise, with our beds always made, floors always perfectly vacuumed, a pot of coffee always ready to be poured, and cupboards stuffed with our favourite treats. As a kid I would play with anything I picked up, and for some reason I was always particularly drawn to her antiques, using seemingly the largest kitchen chair in sight to reach to the top of the china cabinet where they hid waiting for me.

The scent of freshly baked cookies travels from the kitchen as I drift into another world. There's nothing like being a child. Knowing nothing more than that moment right there in front of you. That home was so real, so genuine, oozing with love and care. Just like my grandma.

She was stubborn as stone with a heart of pure gold, she

loved with every piece of herself, her memory lives on in all of us who got the privilege to share a moment with her.

We eventually sold her home that we all loved so much, it took losing the one person that made all those moments so memorable. That's one of the most bittersweet feelings.

Knowing she's not there anymore to keep the light on.

I keep with me the antiques, displayed as a token of my love for her.

When I glance at them, I'm reminded of what home feels like, because she's with me again.

*The funny thing about being in an abusive relationship.
Is that you never realise how suffocated you are being,
Until you can finally.
Breathe again.*

I deserve to be interesting.
I deserve to be wanted and chased.
I deserve to make cool mixtapes with cool songs and make people wonder what my cool mind looks like.
But they don't get to know.
Because its mine.
I want people to see me in a crowd.
See that maybe I am different or unique.
I want someone to love me.
I want someone to think I'm cool.
I want the someone I love to make me feel like my favourite songs.
I made a playlist and I called it fall, not because that is the season but because this is the fall of my existence,
this is the last of my passions and expression.
My music is the last piece of me.
"High and dry" – Radiohead
"Cherry waves" – Deftones
"Fake plastic trees" -Radiohead
"lover, you should have come over" – Jeff Buckley
"lithium" – nirvana
"the bomb" – Florence + the machine
"bohemian rhapsody" – queen
"doin' time" – sublime
"verbatim" – mother mother

"Re: stacks" – bon iver

It is getting cold again, so I cover up.
I add more layers.
More reasons to hide.
My skin, so fragile in the winter.
Do not glance at my scars.
Do not caress this wounded flesh.
Let my body be the garden you cannot enter.
Let me invade your mind with curiosity.
I am your temptress.
Your deepest desire.
That you cannot have.
Because I have become far too busy,
Hating myself. Hurting myself and Deteriorating.
That I cannot fit time to love you.
I cannot distract myself from my flaws.
I cannot waste my love.
I am merely an infatuation.
I am nothing you can hold, nothing tender, nothing sweet, nothing steady.
I am just a figment of your imagination.
Because though I am real.
I am not what you think.
Not what you have painted me to be.
I am cold.
Forever freezing.
But I will no longer cover up.

I've swam in the pools of regret
And laid in the bed of shame
I've shared my lonely nights with lost lovers
And accepted love not fit for anyone with a beating heart.
I've given away parts of myself that I can't remember having now
I've been beaten up by me and the world
I am my own biggest enemy in a place filled with demons.
I can't forgive myself, defend myself, empathize with myself.
Or rationalize anything I do
I hate her.
Look in the fucking mirror.

This body is no longer a vessel to carry your pain.
Nor is it a place to be shamed for the scars it holds
My body does not belong to your mind
Nor your eyes
Or your hands
My body has seen darkness
My body has felt the fear as you tore at my delicate skin
Breaking every boundary
I've seen things.
Now I know.
What I will never allow myself to face again.

Call me what you want- I have heard it all.

But I believe am just looking for love in all the wrong places.

You had a little girl.

You said she was your world.

That the birds sang for her and the flowers bloomed in her presence.

Yet you showed her dark skies and dug her deep beneath the dirt.

You said you would do anything for her.

Would risk everything for her,

But, where were you? Where were you when she was eaten by the world and spat on the curb.

When she was drowned by the rain and evaporated into the sky.

Anything you were meant to teach her.

She had to learn on her own.

She sat alone.

Tears flowing down her face in the night, until the pillow could be rung out.

Comforted by her own sobs.

You were supposed to teach her how to be strong.

But you made her weak.

You were supposed to teach her of her worth.

But you spent all she was.

You beat her into the ground so far, she could no longer grow.

Cornered her with insecurities, humiliated her until she was nothing.

You spat your fallacies of love.

Of her worth.

Of her treasure.

Made her believe you meant every word.

Then you were gone.

Gone until the next time you take what was not yours.

And rid her of every ounce of confidence she had left.

You are cold.

You are heartless and deceitful.

Only in search of self-glorification.

This is how she will always see you.

For your truest colours.

Hoping one day you will see your reflection.

And realise what you have become.

And know that she now hates you just as much as you clearly hate yourself.

1. I'm unplanned. Unwanted.
2. I'm the reason mom can't leave.
3. Mom is crying again. Daddy put a hole in the wall.
4. Moms is left with bruises; daddy is gone again.
5. Sometimes he visits. Mom says he's not allowed in the house anymore.
6. Mom says we have to get away. This is goodbye home.
7. Daddy comes to visit every weekend. We get to play board games in the camper.
8. He didn't tell mom he was coming to get me. I missed her. We sat in silence for most of the weekend.
9. We had to move again. I heard my sister saying he can't know where we live.

    He is not a bad guy. I promise. He is still my superhero.
10. Daddy stopped showing up. I wait for him to pick me up from school.
11. Another home in another city. Sometimes he still calls.
12. I spent Christmas at my dad's. Instead of opening gifts, I close my eyes as he steals the light from hers. It's all a blur.
13. He sent me a card. Says I mean the world to him. I don't believe a word.
14. I have to see him again. I should be happy, but I just want to go home. He is yelling, I'm scared but I bite

bark back. He hits me for the first time and sees me for the last.
15. It's been one year. "you were a mistake."
16. Two years. "you don't deserve my love."
17. Three years. 1095 days. "you're going to be just like me whether you like it or not."
18. Father I hate you.

> Father you broke me.
> Kevin. You are not my father anymore.

My whole life I told myself that I wasn't going to have children,

I hated the thought of seeing another me, another broken thing.

I have this fear that maybe I won't be a good mother.

Perhaps I think I'll never truly find someone that loves me enough to make children with me.

Perhaps it's the deep hatred I carry towards myself and maybe as sinical as it sounds, I would hate my kid for being mine.

Maybe I'm scared that I'll never make enough money, or maybe I will and I'm too selfish to have someone to provide for.

Maybe I'm scared this body isn't ready to bear children, or maybe it shouldn't.

The bad habits I've built will just pass down.

I find myself picturing this fantasy life that I'm so ready to build and its never included a child in the picture.

But last night I caught myself.

Caught myself looking at baby clothes and wishing I could have that one day,

caught myself writing down possible baby names and liking the sound of some over others.

Why do I care now?

How do I even see a future for myself, a year ago this soul

wouldn't have seen herself living past graduation. Now I'm writing down baby names in my notes app.

I still believe this is going to be a lonely life for myself.

I have a hard time believing someone could love me.

I have enough battles to fight withing my mind before I can love.

Before I can move on.

Before I can be free.

Today I sat, sat and thought about time.

Time spent crying, mourning, grieving.

Time I'll never get back.

I look back at old version of myself and wonder if she would like who I've become.

Maybe shed be disappointed. Maybe confused.

I was soft and untouched, now rigid and broken.

Its crazy how time changes and controls our lives.

Over the span of seconds that turned to years I've lost so much hope, so much trust.

If he could break me with such ease, who's to say someone new won't do the same.

Even though I was beaten down and had lost myself. I miss who I was before recovery.

My ending of old habits always leads to new ones.

But I stay standing here

So, time just might have the better of me.

Being young you find safety in the people who hurt you most.
You become so blinded by the pain.
That it disguises as love.
when you grow up,
that pain that is left.
is nothing but a memory.
One day you will see it too,
and you will be so grateful.
You got away.

A child does not choose to hate themselves
We are taught to hate
Taught to shame and oppress
The man in the chair fucked this one up.
Teaching kids to kill themselves because they're too fat, too ugly, too stupid.
We learn negativity before we learn to wipe.
We learn hatred from all the years of evil and darkness before us.
But this generation has a chance.
We don't have to hate ourselves.
What good does it do.
It is so fucking exhausting.

- A superficial world

Suppress what I wish to express
The misconception of needs that aren't met
If I strive for what's best
The further I'm distressed
Forgotten the longing for someone to care
Still feels like a battle
Of something I can't share
You are who you are
But still lies
That you will never be more
I try to believe all the words you feed me
But I'm lured to the feeling of someone who will need me

The love you showed me,
The love that radiates between you and your lover.
That is what I want
That is what I've been dreaming of.
You made me believe.
Its real.
It's everywhere.
Now I feel it too.
You proved I could love myself.
Just as much as you love me.

In the end
Someone is always going to lose
No matter how hard you try to make things work.
Whether it be losing someone you love,
Or losing yourself in loving someone so much,
that you forget who you are.
All good things come to an end.

The boy who raped me.
The boy we must protect.
"He didn't know"
"He was so young"
"What about his future"
What about the future of young girls that need to cover up their shoulders?
that have to buy pocketknives and pepper spray?
The girls that refuse to go out in the dark in fear of the man.
The man that sits on his thrown that we praise.
sitting within his glass castle that we keep shining.
The man at the top that only got there by stepping over the bodies that he broke.
The silent women are what make these men.
The women that broke in the process of making a king.
We stay quiet.
We stay ashamed.
I've even been protecting him from his own wrongdoing.
The world needs to know.
But who's going to tell them.
Who's going to be the one to say his name.
To dig his grave.
To take away all our grievance and pain.

I am all the things that are wrong with me
I am all the bad things I've done
I am my mistakes
I am my flaws
Because I've let those things define me
I allow it to dwell on me in silence
I focus so hard on all the darkness
Tunnel vision.
I can't let go.
I don't want to let go.
Because what if
I don't change.
What if I can't be better than this.

Mother,
I need to reconcile with you
For all the times I have been too cold, too harsh, too angry.
Your heart is golden, you have done everything you could to keep me going.
A single parent balancing the world on her shoulders to support her 3 children.
The worlds back turned to her,
Nobody to reach out a hand.
You have walked through fire and led us blindly through the darkness
To safety.
Yet I find myself shaming you, hurting you and hating you when *my* days are hard.
I am sorry.
I am truly undeniably sorry.
You deserve so much more than *me*.

I am so much more than a sad story.

So much more than the dreadful things that have happened to me.

My body has felt the world.

My mind has embraced the darkness.

There is so much for me to still see, feel, and experience.

The pain is good, and the damage teaches me how to be strong.

No matter how many times you knock me down I will always find a way to get back up.

I will be feared. I will be praised.

I will also be stepped on. And shamed.

The cycle continues.

It just depends on how quickly you can get back up.

I never realised how much they saved my life.
The somber night that was filled with empathy and warmth instead
Of sharp blades intended to take my life.
My life is because of you.
Jasmine
Laila
Taygen
Una
Sarah
Donovan
Kai
Mom
Hannah
Brittany
Derek
Amanda
Aimê
Nick
Jesse
Ayva
Tiana
Sydney

www.ingramcontent.com/pod-product-compliance
Lightning Source LLC
Chambersburg PA
CBHW030305100526
44590CB00012B/527